GREAT ESCAPES

THE KHMER ROUGE

Liz Sonneborn

Marshall Cavendish
Benchmark
New York

D0926853

This publication represents the opinions and views of the author based on
Liz Sonneborn's knowledge and research. The information in this book serves as a general
guide only. The author and publisher have used their best efforts
in preparing this book and disclaim liability rising directly and indirectly from the use and
application of this book.

Other Marshall Cavendish Offices:
Marshall Cavendish International (Asia) Private Limited, 1 New Industrial Road,
Singapore 536196 • Marshall Cavendish International (Thailand) Co Ltd. 253 Asoke, 12th
Flr, Sukhumvit 21 Road, Klongtoey Nua, Wattana, Bangkok 10110, Thailand • Marshall
Cavendish (Malaysia) Sdn Bhd, Times Subang, Lot 46, Subang Hi-Tech Industrial Park,
Batu Tiga, 40000 Shah Alam, Selangor Darul Ehsan, Malaysia

Marshall Cavendish is a trademark of Times Publishing Limited
All websites were available and accurate when this book was sent to press.

Library of Congress Cataloging-in-Publication Data
Sonneborn, Liz. The Khmer Rouge / Liz Sonneborn.
p. cm. — (Great escapes)
Includes bibliographical references and index.
Summary: "Presents accounts of narrow escapes executed by oppressed
individuals and groups while illuminating social issues and the historical background
that led to the atrocities committed in Cambodia's "killing fields"
by the Khmer Rouge"—Provided by publisher.
ISBN 978-1-60870-474-3 (print) — ISBN 978-1-60870-695-2 (ebook)
1. Cambodia—History—1975-1979—Juvenile literature. 2. Parti communiste du
Kampuchea—Juvenile literature. 3. Dith Pran, 1942-2008—Juvenile literature. 4.
Political refugees—Cambodia--Biography—Juvenile literature. 5. Political atrocities—
Cambodia—Juvenile literature. 6. Journalists—Cambodia—Biography—Juvenile
literature. I. Title. II. Series.
DS554.8.S665 2012
959.604'2—dc22
2011005595

Senior Editor: Deborah Grahame-Smith
Publisher: Michelle Bisson
Art Director: Anahid Hamparian
Series Designer: Kay Petronio

Photo research by Linda Sykes
The photographs in this book are used by permission and through the courtesy of: Hulton
Archive/Getty Images: cover, 18, 39; David A. Harvey/National Geographic Images/ Getty
Images: 4; Panoramic Images/Getty Images: 8; Time and Life Pictures/Getty Images: 10;
Altrendo Travel/Getty Images: 12-13; ©Bettmann/Corbis: 20-21; Dith Pran/The New York
Times/Redux: 24, 27, 51, 52; Claude Juvenal/AFP/Getty Images: 29; © Warner Brothers/
Everett Collection: 31; AFP/Getty Images: 34, 63; Topham/The Image Works: 41; Altrendo/
Getty Images: 43; Shaul Schwarz/Getty Images: 46; NYT/The New York Times/Redux: 55;
Mary Evans/Ronald Grant/Everett Collection: 56; Photo by Extraordinary Chamber in the
Courts of Cambodia via Getty Images: 64.

Printed in Malaysia (T)
135642

CONTENTS

The bones of Cambodians killed by the Khmer Rouge regime filled mass graves throughout the areas that became known as the "killing fields."

INTRODUCTION

THE SURVIVOR

In early 1979, Cambodian journalist Dith Pran returned to Siem Reap, the town in which he was born. It was hardly a joyous homecoming. Since he had last been there, the town and its people had been nearly destroyed by the Khmer Rouge, a murderous regime that had ruled over his nation for four bloody years.

In Siem Reap, Dith encountered two women who told him about a grisly discovery they made while searching for firewood in a nearby forest. To confirm their story, he wanted to see what they had seen with his own eyes. Dith convinced the women to take him along as they retraced their path into the forest.

What Dith saw there was later called a "killing field." All around him, the ground was littered with human skulls and other bones, covered only by a thin layer of dirt. Dith later estimated that as many as 5,000 people had been executed outside of Siem Reap.

Among them were many of Dith's own relatives. The women who had taken him to the killing field were at first reluctant to lead him there. They asked him, "Are you afraid of ghosts?" Dith replied, "No, why should I be? The ghosts may be my brothers or sister."

The Brutal Khmer Rouge

The dead had been killed by the Khmer Rouge. This revolutionary group had taken control of Cambodia, a nation in Southeast Asia, in April 1975. During its rule, Khmer Rouge members had been astoundingly brutal to fellow Cambodians. They ruthlessly slaughtered anyone they considered an enemy—even children and babies. Other killing fields like the one Dith discovered were scattered throughout Cambodia.

During the Khmer Rouge era, the Cambodian people suffered horribly. Although the death toll during its reign is disputed, some scholars estimate that as many as 2 million Cambodians, out of a total population of approximately 7 million, died. Many were murdered in the killing fields, but others died of starvation or disease in rural labor camps, where the Khmer Rouge forced them to work. Dith himself had been ordered to work in various villages. Hard labor and severe malnutrition took a toll on his body. His teeth began to fall out, and his hands often shook uncontrollably.

But Dith's mind had remained focused. He vowed that somehow he would keep himself alive long enough to escape Cambodia to freedom.

No Choice but to Escape

Just weeks before Dith returned to Siem Reap, soldiers from the neighboring nation of Vietnam had invaded Cambodia. Their attacks on the Khmer Rouge compelled the Cambodian force to retreat into the jungle. The Khmer Rouge had not gone, but it had lost its complete control over the country. Only then did Dith think that he could flee the labor camp and return to Siem Reap, which had been taken over by Vietnamese troops.

The Vietnamese and the Cambodians were traditional

enemies. Even so, Dith at first felt much safer under the command of the Vietnamese than he had under the Khmer Rouge. But in time, his relationship with the Vietnamese in Siem Reap fell apart. Vietnamese officials seemed to have found out that he had worked as an interpreter for American military personnel and reporters before the rise of the Khmer Rouge. The Vietnamese despised the United States because it had sent military advisers and soldiers into their nation during a long and bloody civil war in the 1960s and early 1970s. Suspecting that the Vietnamese in Siem Reap knew the truth about him, Dith once again feared for his life.

For years, Dith had dreamed of escape. Now the survivor in him believed that he had to try. On July 29, 1979, he sneaked out of Siem Reap and began a treacherous journey. If he was lucky, it would end with him crossing the Cambodian border into neighboring Thailand. If he wasn't lucky, he might meet any of several horrible fates. For example, he might be captured or even killed by roaming Vietnamese troops. He might be attacked by a tiger in the jungle or blown up by a mine concealed underground. Perhaps most of all, Dith feared encountering remnants of the Khmer Rouge army. Now that power was slipping from their grasp, Khmer Rouge soldiers were angry, desperate, and more murderous than ever. And Dith knew, as did anyone who had seen the killing fields, that the Khmer Rouge were capable of anything.

Dith Pran grew up in the town of Siem Reap in northwestern Cambod During his youth, the Cambodian government was controlled by Franc

RISE OF A DANGEROUS REGIME

Dith Pran's story began on September 27, 1942, when he was born in Siem Reap. His father made a good living as an official in charge of constructing roads in the area. He earned enough to build a comfortable home for Dith and his three brothers and two sisters. Dith attended a good school, where he became fluent in French. On his own, he also learned to speak English.

During Dith's youth, Cambodia was not independent. It was instead a protectorate of France. Cambodia's leader, the young king Norodom Sihanouk, had little real power. The government of France had the greatest say in how Cambodia was governed. For many years, however, Sihanouk fought for more control over Cambodia. In 1953, when Dith was eleven years old, Sihanouk negotiated with France to gain Cambodia's independence. Two years later, the popular king won a national election that allowed him to remain the head of state.

The young Cambodian king Norodom Sihanouk, sitting on this throne in 1952.

Not every Cambodian supported Sihanouk. Much of the opposition to his rule came from a group whom the king nicknamed the Khmer Rouge. In French, the name meant "Red Khmer." The Khmer were the largest ethnic group in Cambodia. The color red was associated with communism, the form of government the Khmer Rouge wanted to establish in Cambodia. In a communist nation, the government controls all property and decides how to distribute it to its people. In theory, communism was supposed to create a society in which everyone is treated fairly and equally. In practice, though, large communist-controlled countries in Asia, such as China and the Union of Soviet Socialist Republics (USSR), had very oppressive governments that severely limited their citizens' freedom.

In the late 1950s, the Khmer Rouge was only a small group of would-be revolutionaries hiding out in the Cambodian countryside. Still, its existence alarmed some officials in the United States. At the time, the United States' greatest enemy was the USSR. The United States did not want to see any other nations in Asia become communist and ally themselves with this powerful country. To help Cambodia keep the Khmer Rouge under control, the United States began sending money to Sihanouk's government. Although many Cambodian officials were happy to get their share of U.S. aid, Sihanouk was uneasy with the situation. He believed that accepting the aid might draw Cambodia into a larger conflict involving the powerful United States and USSR.

American Advisers Arrive

For Dith Pran, the United States' interest in Cambodian politics was a boon. After he graduated from high school in 1960, he got a job with the United States' Military Assistance Command. With his knowledge of French, English, and Khmer (the Cambodian language), he was well

THE EARLY HISTORY OF CAMBODIA

The Khmer people, the main ethnic group in Cambodia, had once lived in the great Angkor Empire. This empire reached its peak between the tenth and thirteenth centuries. During the twelfth century, Suryavarman II, the empire's king, built a great complex of temples in the capital city of Angkor.

In the thirteenth century, the Angkor Empire slowly began to decline. In 1431, it was invaded by the Thai people to the northwest, who attacked and destroyed Angkor. Many Khmer people from the capital city then moved south to an area that eventually became Phnom Penh, the capital of Cambodia today.

During the next several centuries, the kings of Cambodia were politically weak. For their own survival, they alternately sought protection from their stronger neighbors, Thailand and Vietnam. In this push-and-pull situation, the two powers gradually chipped land from Cambodia, reducing both its size and influence.

In 1863, another country—France—began seeking control over Cambodia. Threatened by the country's gunboats, King Norodom I was forced to sign a treaty with France that made Cambodia a protectorate controlled by the French government. The country remained under French control until 1953, when it was granted independence.

Cambodia is famous for the spectacular complex of temples at Angkor Wat. Thousands of tourists from around the world visit the temples each year.

qualified to act as an interpreter for this team of American military advisers.

While Dith had this job, American involvement in Vietnam began to heat up. In 1954, the country was split in two—procommunist North Vietnam and anticommunist South Vietnam. Backed by military aid from the United States, South Vietnam went to war against North Vietnam, which wanted to reunite the country as a communist state. The conflict grew into the drawn-out Vietnam War, during which U.S. soldiers fought on the side of South Vietnam. (Despite this support from the United States, North Vietnam won the war in 1975.)

Sihanouk was upset by the escalating conflict. He wanted to keep Cambodia neutral, but that was hard to do if he continued accepting money from the United States. By 1965, Sihanouk had had enough. He accused the U.S. military of launching air attacks on Cambodian villages along the Vietnamese border, and he broke off all diplomatic relations with the United States.

The Khmer Rouge Grows Stronger

Sihanouk's political maneuver cost Dith Pran his job, because the United States had to disband its military assistance group in Cambodia. Dith, however, soon found other work. For a while, he was an interpreter for a British film crew that was making a movie of the classic novel *Lord Jim* in Cambodia. Once the movie wrapped, he became a receptionist at the Auberge Royale des Temples, a large tourist hotel in his hometown. Despite the political upheaval in the region, the nearby temples of Angkor Wat remained a very popular attraction, drawing tourists from around the world.

In the meantime, U.S. air strikes on the Cambodian-Vietnamese border were creating a new crisis in Cambodia. To avoid American bombs, the North Vietnamese soldiers who were stationed there began to move deep into the interior of Cambodia. There, they met members of the Khmer Rouge. Cambodians and Vietnamese traditionally had been enemies, but at least for the moment, they were willing to put aside old grievances. They created a new alliance based on their shared support of communism. The Khmer Rouge had been an unorganized, underfunded revolutionary movement, but it grew quickly after new North Vietnamese allies offered its members military training and weapons purchased from the USSR and China.

The Khmer Rouge was also bolstered by new recruits who opposed General Lon Nol, who became Cambodia's prime minister in 1966. General Nol came down hard on peasants who tried to rebel against Sihanouk's government. His forces beat to death with clubs hundreds of Cambodians. This harsh response created many new opponents to the government— some of whom joined the Khmer Rouge.

The Cambodian Civil War

In March 1970, while Sihanouk was out of the country, Lon Nol staged a military coup and took control of the Cambodian government. A staunch anticommunist, Lon Nol and his new regime were supported by U.S. aid. The United States did not want to see communism spread further in Asia.

Sihanouk was outraged. All of his efforts to keep Cambodia politically neutral had backfired. He now knew that he had to choose a side if he had any chance of reclaiming power. As he explained, "I had chosen not to be with either the Americans or the communists.... It was Lon Nol who obliged me to choose between them." Sihanouk threw his support behind the Khmer Rouge, which was now led by a revolutionary named Pol Pot. Sihanouk was still very popular with many poor Cambodians, especially those in rural areas. He helped to convince them that the Khmer Rouge was made

"BRIGHT FIRE ON THE EARTH"

In her memoir, *When Broken Glass Floats,* Cambodian writer Chanrithy Him described the terror she felt as a girl when American troops bombed her village:

Something drops down loudly. The house shakes. I open my eyes. It drops again and again as if a big fist were pounding on the ground. Gigantic tongues of fire and smoke lick the black sky, lighting up the landscape in the distance. Silhouettes of planes loop in the darkness with sequins of light pouring from them. The sequins dissipate in the brushy shadow of distant trees, then erupt in enormous explosions, bright fire on the earth. We see it before we hear it, the explosion arriving as a delayed echo. Each burst concludes with a huge mushroom of smoke.

"Pa?" I squeeze my father's hand, looking up
at the shadow of his face.
Never before have I seen men cry, so much,
like *Pa* tonight.

up of patriotic Cambodians trying to save their country from the corrupt Lon Nol government and the American military forces who were bombing their villages.

Lon Nol's coup and Sihanouk's defiance plunged Cambodia into a civil war. The conflict was further complicated by foreign interference. The Americans and South Vietnamese sided with Lon Nol, while the Soviets (people of the USSR) and the North Vietnamese sided with Sihanouk and the Khmer Rouge.

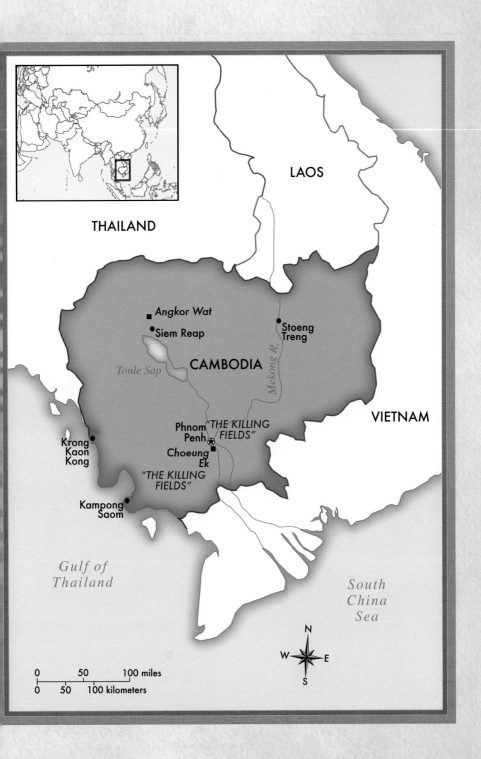

LAOS

THAILAND

Angkor Wat

Siem Reap

Stoeng
Treng

CAMBODIA

Tonle Sap

Mekong R.

VIETNAM

Phnom "THE KILLING
Penh FIELDS"

Krong
Kaon
Kong

Choeung
Ek

"THE KILLING
FIELDS"

Kampong
Saom

Gulf of
Thailand

South
China
Sea

0   50   100 miles
0   50   100 kilometers

N
W   E
S

Lon Nol staged a military takeover of the Cambodian government in March 1970. His
regime, which was staunchly
anticommunist, was supported
by the United States.

Once again, the changing political atmosphere of Cambodia had personal consequences for Dith Pran. He lost his job at the Auberge Royale des Temples when the hotel was destroyed by the Viet Cong, a communist faction of South Vietnamese soldiers. Dith left Siem Reap and headed to Phnom Penh, the capital of Cambodia. With Cambodia engulfed in a civil war, he knew that foreign diplomats and reporters were heading toward the city. With his experience, he was sure he could land a job there as an interpreter.

Dith first tried to find work at the American embassy, the complex of buildings that housed the American ambassador to Cambodia and his staff. Although the embassy was expanding, it was not yet ready to hire new employees. While waiting for an embassy job, Dith worked part-time for various newspapers, including the *New York Times,* one of the most prestigious newspapers in the United States.

Working for the *Times*

In September 1972, Dith waited at the Pochentong Airport in Phnom Penh to meet Sydney Schanberg, a new *Times* correspondent he was assigned to work with. As soon as Schanberg got off the plane, Dith presented him with a notebook full of observations about things he had seen and heard. He also had a list of people whom he thought Schanberg should talk with. Even though Dith had no training as a journalist, he was developing a keen interest in reporting. He wanted to be more than an interpreter. He wanted to be a journalistic partner whose knowledge of his people and his country would prove invaluable to Schanberg's work.

Schanberg quickly recognized Dith's talents and drive. So did several other foreign reporters, who tried to lure Dith into working for them. To make sure he did not lose Dith to the competition, Schanberg arranged for the *Times* to hire Dith on a permanent basis and pay him a monthly salary.

Drawing a regular paycheck was a welcome relief to Dith, who now had a wife, Ser Moeun, and four children. The secure income also freed him to concentrate on his work and mission—to help Schanberg report on the troubles of his beloved country.

Dith saw that many foreign reporters had no idea how to interview ordinary Cambodians. Through interpreters, they would ask probing questions that put people off. Dith developed a gentler, subtler approach: "I'd give the soldier a cigarette, ask

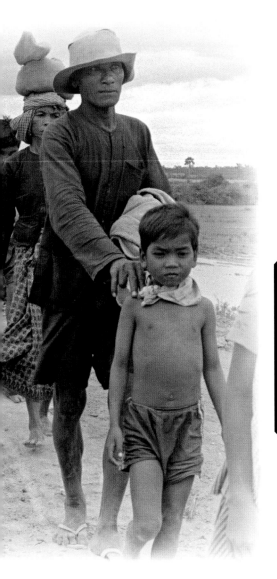

As the Cambodian civil war intensified in early 1975, many rural Cambodians left their homes to escape the fighting and sought refuge in the capital city of Phnom Penh.

him: 'How are you? What's it like here? What's happening?' Make him happy, and he'd talk and talk. And Sydney knew what I was doing. He and I had the same idea."

The Khmer Rouge Closes In

Dith's job became more intense and dangerous as the civil war continued. He and Schanberg spent their days dashing from place to place, trying to figure out what was going on in an increasingly chaotic world. Often they stayed up all night working, with Schanberg frantically hammering out his reports on a typewriter and Dith pleading with cable operators to send his stories to New York as quickly as possible so that they could meet their deadlines with the *Times*. The articles helped bring international attention to the crisis in Cambodia.

The pressures of the job were hard on Dith, but even more distressing was watching his country deteriorate. Years of war were taking a terrible toll on the Cambodian people. Bombings had forced many rural workers to abandon their fields and rice paddies, which in turn led to severe food shortages. Every day, Dith saw more refugees from the countryside crowding into Phnom Penh. In time, the population of the capital quadrupled from about 500,000 before the outbreak of the war to almost 2 million.

Many of the refugees told terrible stories about how the Khmer Rouge was brutalizing anyone whom they believed opposed their cause. All the while, the Khmer Rouge was growing larger and stronger. At the same time, the army of Lon Nol's government was becoming weaker. Many of its leaders were corrupt. They took military aid provided by the United States, but instead of using it to hire more soldiers, they simply put the money in their own pockets.

The United Nations, an international organization dedicated to promoting world peace, tried to bring the two factions together to end the war in Cambodia. But with the Khmer Rouge becoming more convinced that it could take over the entire country, its leaders flatly refused to negotiate.

As the Khmer Rouge gained strength, it moved out of the countryside and toward Phnom Penh. Dith's life grew even more frantic, as he and Schanberg raced through the city trying to find out everything they could about the Khmer Rouge soldiers' progress. As focused as Dith was on getting out the day's news, he could not stop thinking about the future. If the Khmer Rouge did make it to the capital and were able to take over the government, he wondered, what would happen next?

This photograph of Dith Pran was taken in April 1970, when the Khmer Rouge takeover of Phnom Penh left everyone in the capital on edge about Cambodia's future.

TWO

SEEKING REFUGE

Early on the morning of April 12, 1975, Dith Pran was abruptly woken by a messenger from Sydney Schanberg. Up until three o'clock in the morning working, Dith was still groggy as he took in the messenger's news. The American embassy in Phnom Penh had made a sudden decision. In just a few hours, it was going to evacuate its staff by helicopter. The Khmer Rouge was getting closer to the city, and the embassy no longer thought Phnom Penh was safe for Americans.

Dith had known that this day might come. He and Schanberg had talked about it. Because they were employees for an American newspaper, the American embassy would have agreed to help them leave the country. But neither of them wanted to leave. Each believed he had a duty to stay and report on the new regime. No matter how dangerous the situation might be, Schanberg felt an obligation to his newspaper; Dith, to his country.

With Schanberg's help, however, Dith had arranged for the embassy to evacuate Ser Moeun and his children to the United States, if conditions warranted it. Now he had to act quickly to make sure they got out before the Khmer Rouge reached the city. Immediately, he gathered his family and helped them pack the few bags they could carry. They all piled into his old car and raced to the embassy.

Just ten minutes before the evacuation ended, Dith's car pulled up to the embassy gates. The scene was chaotic. Crowds of Cambodians clamored to get inside. Guards would open the gates only for employees or those who had connections to the embassy. Everyone else was turned away.

Schanberg was outside the embassy, and he rushed to meet Dith. Even though they had discussed the situation before, he again asked Dith whether he wanted to escape with his family. Without hesitation, Dith said no. Ser Moeun was distraught. She begged her husband to come with her. Dith assured her that he would be safe. After all, he was smart enough to figure out how to handle himself in any situation. Still upset, she and the children scrambled into a flatbed truck filled with other evacuees. Dith and Schanberg stood silently as the truck drove away toward the helicopter landing.

Waiting for the Khmer Rouge

After the last helicopter took off, the streets of Phnom Penh were eerily quiet. It was as though its 2 million residents were holding their breath, all waiting uneasily for what was to come. But for Dith and Schanberg, it was time to get to work. They ran from hospitals to government offices to any place else where they thought they could get a scrap of news. They spent their nights at the cable office, sending off stories whenever its employees could get its electric generator to work. For days, they survived on only a few hours of sleep. They did not even take time to change their clothes.

On April 12, 1975, Cambodians watch as a helicopter lands near the U.S. embassy to help Americans there escape from the country. (This photo was taken by Dith Pran.)

On the night of April 16, the Khmer Rouge reached Phnom Penh. Outside the cable office, the sky was orange from the light of explosions. The streets filled with rural refugees trying to escape the bombs. They marched wearily alongside members of Lon Nol's army who were deserting a cause they now saw as lost. Dith and Schanberg looked at each other, each seeing his own anxiety mirrored on the other's face. "It's finished, it's finished," Dith said quietly.

Across the city, residents hung white sheets outside their windows to show the approaching soldiers that they were prepared to surrender to their will. Everyone was nervous, but some people still held out hope. Maybe life under the Khmer Rouge would not be so bad, they thought. At least Cambodia would no longer be at war.

When the Khmer Rouge showed up in the streets, however, their manner alarmed even the optimists. According to Schanberg, "They [were] universally grim, robotlike, brutal. Weapons drip[ped] from them like fruit from trees—grenades, pistols, rifles, rockets." Most were young men. Many were barely in their teens.

Even the youngest members of the Khmer Rouge had seen terrible things during the civil war. The Lon Nol regime had brutally killed many Khmer Rouge, and memories of these murders fueled their hatred of the corrupt government. Their experiences traumatized them and taught them to embrace violence. When the Khmer Rouge won the war, Pol Pot and other leaders wanted to take full advantage of the psychological damage caused by years of war. By encouraging the soldiers to inflict the cruelest violence on the Khmer Rouge's enemies, the leaders hoped to eliminate all opposition forces and to cow all other Cambodians into giving them complete power without question.

Dith and Schanberg approached one of the soldiers. Dith chatted with the man, and Schanberg offered him a cigarette. The friendly conversation made the soldier drop his guard, and for a moment, he smiled. Schanberg had Dith ask him whether the Khmer Rouge was planning on killing a large number of people after it took charge. Dith translated his ominous words: "Those who have done corrupt things will definitely have to be punished."

Only hours after arriving, the Khmer Rouge announced its plans. All the people in Phnom Penh—2 million residents—

The rank and file of the Khmer Rouge celebrate as they storm into Phnom Penh after the group's takeover of the Cambodian national government.

were to leave the city and march into the countryside. The Khmer Rouge told them that the order was for their own safety. They claimed that American troops were about to bomb the city—a lie that nevertheless was believable to most Cambodians because U.S. troops had previously bombed parts of the country. Through megaphones, Khmer Rouge leaders also announced that officials of the defeated Lon Nol government should report to the Information Ministry. The Khmer Rouge assured the officials that they would be treated fairly.

Taken Captive

Dith and Schanberg rushed to the Preah Keth Mealea hospital. With few doctors, and with many patients injured in the recent fighting, the building was full of the dead and dying. But even the injured and ill had to follow the Khmer Rouge's orders. British journalist Jon Swain described the evacuation of the patients: "Bandaged men and women hobble[d] by the embassy. Wives push[ed] wounded soldier husbands on hospital beds on wheels, some with serum drips still attached. In five years of war, this [was] the greatest caravan of human misery I have seen."

Dith, Schanberg, their driver, and two other journalists left the hospital together. As soon as they got in their cars, a band of Khmer Rouge soldiers forced them at gunpoint to get out. Dith insisted, "We are not fighters, we are international press," hoping that would persuade the Khmer Rouge to leave them alone. He also lied to the soldiers, claiming that everyone in the group was French. Dith knew the Khmer Rouge hated Americans because of their support for the Lon Nol government.

Despite Dith's pleading, the soldiers ordered the reporters to put their hands on their heads, and they herded them into an armored truck. Dith remained outside, speaking quickly and frantically in Khmer to the soldiers. Schanberg could not understand his words, but he figured that Dith was asking them to let him go. Actually, Dith was begging the soldiers to allow him to join them on the truck. Dith suspected that the Khmer Rouge would kill the foreign journalists, even if they bought the idea that they were French and not American. Although it put Dith at risk of death, he talked his way onto the truck so that he could continue to plead their case.

For a while, as the truck drove around the city, Dith kept talking to the driver, saying whatever he thought might convince him to release the prisoners. Finally, the truck stopped, and the captives were ordered out of the truck. Dith continued to talk, while the others stood terrified as several gunmen guarded them.

Dith quickly sized up the situation. He spotted one Khmer Rouge soldier with a clean uniform and guessed that he was in charge because the most important leaders always seemed to carry the largest number of pens. Dith focused his pleas on the officer. After an hour of constant begging, the soldiers seemed to soften. They gave Dith and the others a drink of water and let them move out of the hot sun and into the shade. Finally, the soldiers released them, but not without first rifling through their bags and backpacks, looking for

Haing S. Ngor played Dith Pran and Sam Waterston portrayed Sydney Schanberg in *The Killing Fields*, the popular film that dramatized the two men's experiences in Cambodia during the Khmer Rouge era.

valuables they could steal. Only by chance did they not notice the reporters' passports, official government documents that stated their citizenship. If the Khmer Rouge had looked at their passports, they would have realized Dith was lying when he said they were French. For that alone, the Khmer Rouge might have executed them all.

At the French Embassy

Determined to continue their reporting, Dith and Schanberg headed to the Information Ministry, where about fifty government officials had gathered. Among them was Long Boret, the prime minister under Lon Nol. Both Dith and Schanberg shook his hand, and Schanberg told him he was brave to stay behind to try to negotiate with the Khmer Rouge rather than leaving with the Americans when he had a chance. Long Boret looked grim, even when Schanberg paid him the compliment. All three men were sure that Boret was about to be killed.

By the late afternoon, Dith and Schanberg made their way back to the Hotel Le Phnom, where Schanberg had a room. The hotel was almost empty because the Khmer Rouge had ordered everyone out. With no time to think, they rushed back into the street and raced toward the French embassy, about a half-mile (1 kilometer) away. By then, the embassy was the only place in Cambodia that was safe for foreigners. At the end of the day, some 800 foreigners and 600 of their Cambodian friends and associates found sanctuary there. The embassy officials let the foreigners into its four buildings, but the Cambodians were forced to camp outside on the grounds. After sunset, however, Schanberg sneaked Dith inside.

The next day, the French officials told everyone at the embassy to turn over their passports. The order seemed to confirm a disturbing rumor: The French were negotiating to evacuate the foreigners, but the Cambodians at the embassy would be left to fend for themselves. Two Cambodian drivers who had worked for Schanberg then decided to leave on their own. They thought they would have better luck if they tried to blend in with the rest of the Cambodians evacuating Phnom Penh. It was becoming clear that the Khmer Rouge was not going to be kind to any Cambodian who was known to have had close ties to an American. Dith, though, decided to stay, and Schanberg hatched a plan to get him evacuated with the foreigners. Jon Swain had a second passport. Dith's friends doctored the passport so that he could use it. The French, however, immediately spotted the passport as a forgery. They pulled Schanberg aside and told him that the trick would never work. Schanberg told Dith what had happened and gave him $2,600, which he hoped Dith could use as bribe money in dealing with the Khmer Rouge. The next morning, the two men stood outside the embassy gate. They hugged one another, but neither said a word. Then Dith, with a small bag in hand, turned and took his place in the seemingly endless stream of Cambodians cast out of their capital city.

After the Khmer Rouge took control of the Cambodian government in April 1975, many people in the capital of Phnom Penh were forced to leave the city and travel with whatever they could carry to the countryside.

THREE

THE KILLING FIELDS

The exodus out of the capital was a parade of misery. The road was littered with shoes that had slipped off the migrants' feet while they were chided by Khmer Rouge soldiers to move more quickly. Soldiers taunted even the elderly and ailing, many of whom were being carried on the backs of their loved ones. If the Khmer Rouge felt any human sympathy for the evacuees' plight, they did not show it. Any resistance to their demands was met with swift and sure punishment. Dith saw the Khmer Rouge soldiers order one young man to surrender his motorbike to them. When he refused, one yelled, "You're a traitor, that motorbike belongs to the people and to our leadership, not to you!" They then tied him up and beat him while his horrified family looked on.

The Khmer Rouge were even more brutal to people who refused to leave their homes and join the march. They were all murdered. The soldiers' actions sent a message: Anyone who dared defy them could expect to die.

A New Identity

Dith realized that he would have to deceive the Khmer Rouge if he had any hope of surviving. The Khmer Rouge was not only targeting Cambodians with connections to the Lon Nol government and Americans and other foreigners. It also hated professors, teachers, and anyone else who had an education or an urban background. As an educated city dweller who had worked for an American newspaper, Dith personified much that the Khmer Rouge hated. He wisely decided to become someone else. Dith carefully created a new identity for himself. He ditched his old clothes and put on a dirty shirt, shorts, and sandals—the clothing a poor person from rural Cambodia would wear. He threw away the bribe money Schanberg had given him. The U.S. dollars could have revealed his American ties—and besides, in the new Cambodia, money was worthless anyway. Dith passed himself off as a humble taxi driver by changing the way he spoke and acted. He became very quiet and meek. He spoke as little as possible, and he used only simple words that would not betray his schooling. Dith later explained his strategy: "To survive, you have to pretend to be stupid, because they don't want you to be smart. They think that smart people will destroy them."

Dith hoped to return to his hometown of Siem Reap, where he could be reunited with his mother, father, and siblings. But when he reached the village of Dam Dek, he changed his mind. Dam Dek was only 20 miles (32 km) from Siem Reap. But there, he heard rumors that the Khmer Rouge soldiers in Siem Reap were especially cruel. Reluctantly, he asked the Khmer Rouge authorities for permission to stay in Dam Dek.

Goals of the New Regime

Settled in Dam Dek, Dith first experienced the kind of world the Khmer Rouge hoped to create. According to its communist ideals, social classes in Cambodia would no longer exist.

All Cambodians were to be of one class: the rural working class that labored day after day in fields and rice paddies. People would no longer have ties to religions, communities, or even families. Every institution, whether it was a bank, a church, or a university, was considered corrupt. From now on, Cambodians would have only one loyalty—to the Khmer Rouge. In an effort to erase the old Cambodia from the people's minds, Khmer Rouge leaders renamed the country Democratic Kampuchea. They also did everything they could to isolate Kampuchea. The Khmer Rouge made sure that no one outside the country knew what was going on inside Cambodia and that no one in Cambodia received any news from the rest of the world.

In its mania to re-create Cambodia completely, the Khmer Rouge also touted the concept of Year Zero. Its leaders said that the past was unimportant. The year that the Khmer Rouge rose to power—1975—in essence marked a restarting of history's clock. Everything that happened before was to be forgotten.

From this notion, it naturally followed that all adults were corrupt because they still had memories of a world before the Year Zero. As a result, the Khmer Rouge embraced teenagers and even welcomed children into its ranks. With fewer memories, children could more easily be molded to accept without question the Khmer Rouge's world view. The Khmer Rouge encouraged children to inform on adults, especially their relatives. As a show of loyalty, children were sometimes forced to kill their teachers—or even their own parents.

Always under the watchful eye of the Khmer Rouge, Cambodians from all walks of life were forced to become farm laborers. Every day, they woke up very early to begin work. Depending on the season, they might spend as many as fourteen hours in the fields or rice paddies. At night, they were required to attend meetings, during which the Khmer Rouge "reeducated" them. In these sessions, Cambodians were told to forget their old lives and to become loyal servants of the Khmer Rouge. As Dith once explained, serving the regime meant obeying its leaders, no matter what they demanded. "What they were really telling us was, never refuse an order, never complain, never say you haven't got enough food, just listen to what the Angka, the leadership, tells you to do."

Under the Khmer Rouge, even the bonds of love and family were held under suspicion. People were told to put the Khmer Rouge first in their hearts, before their parents, spouses, and children. To help destroy personal ties, the regime routinely separated families. Children were often sent to different labor camps than those where their parents were housed. Sometimes these family members never saw one another again.

Work crews were segregated by gender, so wives and husbands in the same camp saw little of one another. The Khmer Rouge also forced many men and women into arranged marriages. At mass weddings, the leaders married hundreds of couples at a time. Some young people killed themselves rather than allow the Khmer Rouge to marry them to a stranger.

Destroying All Enemies

Soon after taking power, the Khmer Rouge began murdering everyone connected with the Lon Nol government, as well as teachers, doctors, scientists, and anyone else who had an education. Many of these suspected opponents of the regime were sent to Tuol Sleng, a high school in Phnom Penh that had been turned into an interrogation center called S-21. The center was run by a former high school teacher named Kaing Guek Eav. Cambodians jailed there were tortured until they confessed that they were enemies of the state. Of the approximately 14,000 people interrogated at S-21, only a handful survived the ordeal.

The Khmer Rouge "reeducated" Cambodia's children by telling them to forget their past lives and offer their complete obedience to the new regime. Anyone who defied the Khmer Rouge leaders was punished or even killed.

CHILDREN AND THE KHMER ROUGE

Years after the Khmer Rouge era, Dith Pran recorded the stories of about thirty Cambodian adults who had been children during the Khmer Rouge's reign. These memories were collected in *Children of Cambodia's Killing Fields: Memoirs by Survivors* (1997). In this excerpt, a woman named Seath K. Teng recalled the horrors she saw during that time.

At the age of four I was robbed of my normal childhood. I was separated from my family to face the cruelty and hatred of the Khmer Rouge. The Khmer Rouge soldiers told us not to love our parents or to depend on them because they are not the ones who supported us. If we didn't do as they said, we would get a severe beating for punishment.

I remember that we did most of the jobs in the rice field. We grew so much rice, but they fed us so little. We worked seven days a week without a break. The only time we got off work was to see someone get killed, which served as an example for us. I can still remember one of these killings vividly.

In the center of the meeting place was one woman who had both her hands tied behind her. She was pregnant and her stomach bulged out. Before her stood a little boy who was about six years old and holding an ax. In his shrill voice, he yelled for us to look at what he was going to do. He said if we didn't look, we would be the next to be killed. I guess we all looked, because the woman was the only one killed that day. The little boy was like a demon from hell. His eyes were red and he didn't look human at all. He used the back of his ax and slammed it hard on the poor woman's body until she dropped to the ground. He kept beating her until he was too tired to continue.

Out of fear for their lives, many young soldiers committed atrocious acts of violence in service of the Khmer Rouge regime.

In the rural labor camps, the Khmer Rouge continued to kill anyone perceived as an enemy. One could be targeted for death for even the slightest infraction, such as taking a break from work without permission. A man and woman not married by the Khmer Rouge who were caught holding hands could also expect a death sentence. Often the soldiers killed people for no reason at all. As Dith once said, "Anyone they didn't like, they would accuse of being a teacher or a student or a former Lon Nol soldier, and that was the end." The killings took place at night, a distance away from where the workers slept. The Khmer Rouge usually murdered their victims by beating them with sticks or farm tools to save money on bullets.

The Khmer Rouge's wrath was not the only danger that Cambodians faced in the countryside. In the work camps, diseases spread rapidly. Malaria was particularly common. By early 1976, as much as 80 percent of Cambodia's population had contracted the disease.

Many others died of starvation. The Khmer Rouge had predicted that it would increase the annual production of rice, the main food crop in Cambodia, by three times after it came to power. Ironically, though, its agricultural experiments were a disaster. The Khmer Rouge distrusted all technology, so its officials rejected modern agricultural knowledge and instead revived centuries-old farming methods. It also tried to farm varieties of rice provided by its Chinese allies, but the Chinese rice did not grow well in Cambodia. In addition, some scholars believe that the Khmer Rouge was exporting to China a large portion of the rice it was able to harvest, in exchange for weapons. As a result, under the Khmer Rouge, Cambodia experienced widespread famine. Workers had to get by on one watery bowl of rice a day, and sometimes even less.

People constantly scavenged for anything that would

The Khmer Rouge transformed a former high school into S-21, a prison also known as Tuol Sleng. There, perceived enemies to the regime were tortured within these doored booths.

supplement their tiny food rations. They ate snails, insects, rats, snakes, and lizard eggs. They even caught and roasted scorpions, despite the threat of their deadly sting.

Struggling to Survive

The famine struck Dam Dek hard. At one point, Dith received a ration of only one spoon of rice a day. He became so weak that he could no longer stand without leaning on a stick. One night, after the Khmer Rouge guards were asleep, Dith sneaked into a rice paddy and began picking out a few kernels to eat. When two guards caught him, he tried to run away, but his legs crumpled beneath him.

The Khmer Rouge tied his hands behind his back and led him out of the camp. Ten men and two women began pounding him with tools used to cut bamboo, yelling, "You are the enemy. You were stealing rice from the collective." Dith was afraid they might beat him to death or cut off his head. But he was still alive when they left him. He spent the next night in the rain, bound like an animal.

The Khmer Rouge leaders at Dam Dek chose not to execute Dith. One convinced the others to allow him to live because he was a good worker. Instead, they paraded him in front of the other workers at the camp, and they made him swear never again to break any rules. A devout Buddhist, Dith showed his gratitude for his survival in the traditional manner, by cutting off his hair. He had to hide this religious act from the Khmer Rouge, however. Dith made up a story that he had been having terrible headaches and that he thought shaving his head might provide some relief.

Dith remained in Dam Dek for more than two years. But by the end of 1977, he came to believe that he could not survive there for much longer. The Khmer Rouge was beginning to fall apart. Just as its officials distrusted outsiders, they began to distrust each other. They began to break into factions, each of which feared all the other factions. These tensions made every member in the Khmer Rouge more paranoid than ever. The number of executions spiked as the Khmer Rouge became more suspicious and desperate. When Dith found out that some people at Dam Dek were saying he could not be trusted, he knew it was only a matter of time before the Khmer Rouge came after him.

Dith asked for permission to move to the nearby village of Bat Dangkor. He had heard that the leaders there were becoming disillusioned with the Khmer Rouge movement and were not nearly as violent as those in Dam Dek. Happily for Dith, the rumors proved true. Even better, in Bat Dangkor he became a favorite of a leader named Phat, who protected him from the more militant Khmer Rouge members. As Dith later recalled, "[Phat] loved me like a brother and took me to work for him in his house, looking after his three children and doing the cleaning." Although he "was like a slave" in Phat's household, he no longer had to worry whether each day was going to be his last.

The Vietnamese Invasion

Living in Phat's house had another benefit: Phat had a radio. Once a week, Dith secretly listened to radio news on the Voice of America, a broadcasting service operated by the U.S. government. From it, he learned that the Khmer Rouge and Vietnamese armies were fighting along the Cambodia-Vietnam border throughout much of 1978. Traditionally, Vietnam and Cambodia had been enemies, and Pol Pot and the other Khmer Rouge leadership, overestimating their power, had decided to challenge their long-hated foes. The news of the skirmishes gave Dith hope. Maybe the Vietnamese could defeat the hated Khmer Rouge and drive them from his country once and for all.

In the final days of 1978, the Vietnamese troops crossed the border into Cambodia and quickly swept through the country.

A Khmer Rouge survivor holds a picture of herself from the days before she was imprisoned and tortured by the regime.

"MY SPIRIT AND MY SOUL HAD RETURNED"

In an essay in *Children of Cambodia's Killing Fields*, a woman named Teeda Butt Mam described the emotions she felt when the Khmer Rouge lost control of Cambodia.

> When the Vietnamese invasion happened, I cried. I was crying with joy that my life was saved. I was crying with sorrow that my country was once again invaded by our century-old enemy. I traveled with my family from the heart of the country to the border of Thailand. It was devastating to witness the destruction of my homeland that had occurred in only four years. This destruction was tolerable compared to the human conditions. Each highway was filled with refugees. We were refugees of our own country. With our skinny bodies, bloated stomachs, and hollow eyes, we carried our few possessions and looked for our separated family members. We asked who lived and didn't want to mention who died.
>
> In April 1979, the Buddhist New Year, exactly four years after the Khmer Rouge came to power, I joined a group of corpselike bodies dancing freely to the sound of clapping and songs of folk music that defined who we were. We danced under the moonlight around the bonfire. We were celebrating the miracles that saved our lives. At that moment, I felt that my spirit and my soul had returned to my weak body. Once again, I was human.

From the beginning, they had the Khmer Rouge on the run. As the Khmer Rouge soldiers retreated, the Vietnamese took control of Phnom Penh. Just two weeks after they launched their invasion, the Vietnamese established a new government in the capital and renamed the country the People's Republic of Kampuchea. Dith was thrilled by the news. At last, the Khmer Rouge era was finally over.

Returning Home

Dith decided to leave Bat Dangkor and return to Siem Reap. Along the way, he saw many others headed toward the town. "All the refugees looked terrible, they were starving....It was very crowded and most people looked like they came from Hell." Dith met one girl who was still in her teens but had the face of a middle-aged woman. She had been in the Battambang region, which had been particularly hard-hit by famine. She told Dith that some people there survived by digging up recently buried corpses and eating their flesh.

A few miles from Siem Reap, Dith ran into his mother and one of his sisters. He was so thin and weak that his sister barely recognized him. After a tearful reunion, they told Dith some horrible news. About fifty of his relatives had died. Among the deceased were his father, his three brothers, one of his sisters, and most of his nieces and nephews. Dith's situation was not unique. Many Cambodians had returned to their homes only to find that nearly everyone in their families had been killed.

When Dith arrived in Siem Reap, his old friends and neighbors were stunned to see him. Given his background, they had assumed he was one of the earliest victims of the Khmer Rouge. They lobbied for the Vietnamese to name Dith the administrative chief of Siem Reap, a position similar to mayor. The people of Siem Reap respected Dith, and as one of the few educated Cambodians in the area, he seemed a natural choice. Dith was hesitant, but he agreed to take the job so he could help his people. His Vietnamese superiors liked him and listened when he asked for food and clothing for the suffering refugees.

A few months later, Dith noticed a change in their attitudes. He suspected that someone told the Vietnamese officials that he had once worked for Americans. The Vietnamese forced Dith to resign his position. But he feared the matter would not end there. Dith had long hoped to escape from Cambodia, but he had been waiting for the right opportunity. Waiting, though, was no longer an option. If he wanted to stay alive, he would have to make his move now.

A Daring Escape

On July 29, 1979, Dith left Siem Reap without telling anyone of his plans. He traveled to the village of Phum Trom about 40 miles (64 km) away. He had heard that an anticommunist group called Sereika (meaning "liberation") was stationed there. Sereika was helping people leave Cambodia by crossing the border into Thailand. In Phum Trom, Dith met other Cambodians who wanted to flee. Together, they spent several weeks plotting their escape.

By the middle of September, they were ready. Dith and eleven other men headed along a winding, 60-mile (96.5-km) trail that would take them over steep hills and through a jungle. All the while, they had to steer clear both of Khmer Rouge soldiers and Vietnamese troops. Either group might kill them if they discovered them.

On the second day of their flight, the men were walking along the trail in single file with Dith third in line when suddenly there was an explosion. One of the men in front of Dith had stepped on a land mine. A bit of metal hit Dith's torso, but the injury was minor. The two men at the head of the line, however, were blown to bits.

Two days later, the surviving members of the group made it to the Thai border. Thailand had been known to reject Cambodian refugees and force them to turn around. However, all the men except for Dith had contacts in Thailand who would protect them from authorities. They all entered Thailand, leaving only Dith behind. With freedom almost in his grasp, Dith stayed in Cambodia for seventeen days as he tried to figure out a scheme to slip into Thailand safely. Finally, on October 3, he came up with a plan. Friends gave him a uniform like those worn by members of Sereika. The Sereika regularly moved in and out of Thailand for medicine and other supplies, so Dith reasoned that if he wore the uniform, he might be able to sneak in without drawing too much attention. Marshaling all the courage he could, he donned the uniform and walked over the border. No one stopped him.

Dith made his way to a refugee camp and looked for someone to help him. He approached an American relief worker, told her his story, and asked her to contact the American embassy in Thailand. He hoped the embassy could get word of his situation to Schanberg.

Dith waited nervously in the camp. He tried to keep a low profile because he still feared that Thai authorities might send him back over the border. On October 9, a friend in the camp rushed into the hut where he was sleeping. "An American brother has come to see you," he said. Dith walked outside and saw Schanberg standing before him. He ran to greet his old friend and literally jumped into his arms. As both men wept, Dith declared, "I am reborn. This is my second life."

Sydney Schanberg and Dith Pran delight in seeing one another during their reunion in Thailand in October 1979.

Having just escaped to safety in Thailand, Dith Pran, with a wide smile, shows his relief in getting out of Cambodia alive.

FOUR

TELLING THE WORLD

With the help of the American embassy in Thailand, Dith was placed at the top of the list of Cambodian refugees seeking a new life in the United States. While waiting for his paperwork to come through, he and Schanberg moved into a hotel in the city of Bangkok. For Dith, readjusting to the outside world was difficult after living through the nightmare of the Khmer Rouge regime. Buying clothes in a department store, eating a stack of pancakes for breakfast, sleeping in a bed between clean white sheets—all these everyday acts seemed remarkable after years of horror and deprivation.

Slowly, Dith became more comfortable in his new surroundings, but he found it hard to talk about the Khmer Rouge. When he told Schanberg what had happened to him, he spoke only in whispers. He was still so fearful of the Khmer Rouge that he was instinctively nervous that he would be overheard and then punished for speaking ill of the hated regime.

Sharing Dith's Story

Schanberg also told Dith what he had been doing since they had last seen each other. After making sure that Dith's family was safely settled in San Francisco, California, Schanberg desperately searched for information about Dith. He sent out more than one hundred letters to his contacts in the United States and throughout Asia asking for help. Schanberg had received the Pulitzer Prize, the most prestigious award in American journalism, for his reportage on the fall of Phnom Penh. In his acceptance speech, he spoke movingly about Dith, acknowledging that without him, he could not have written the award-winning articles.

On October 19, 1979, Dith finally boarded a plane for San Francisco, where he was reunited with his family. His children had grown so much during their four years apart that he barely recognized them. Three months later, they all resettled in Brooklyn, New York, after Dith took a job as a photographer with the *New York Times*. Dith had occasionally taken news photographs in Cambodia, but he had not received formal training in photography. Now, learning the trade under the tutelage of some of the best news photographers in the world, Dith mastered the profession. During his twenty-seven-year career with the *Times,* Dith was recognized particularly for his city scenes and human interest photographs.

Dith also became well known for his efforts to tell the world what happened to Cambodia and its people during the Khmer Rouge reign. Traveling throughout the United States, he delivered lectures about his experiences and spoke out against repressive governments worldwide. Dith's story was also publicized by Schanberg in an in-depth article, "The Death

After leaving Cambodia, Dith Pran found a new life working as a photographer for the *New York Times* alongside his friend and colleague Sydney Schanberg.

A POWERFUL STORY OF FRIENDSHIP, HONOUR AND A FLIGHT TO FREEDOM ON THE BATTLEFIELDS OF CAMBODIA.

THE KILLING FIELDS

RNATIONAL FILM INVESTORS present AN ENIGMA PRODUCTION
WATERSTON · Dr. HAING S. NGOR   Music by MIKE OLDFIELD
ON Produced by DAVID PUTTNAM   Directed by ROLAND JOFFÉ
BLE ON RECORDS & TAPES   DOLBY STEREO

The story of Dith Pran's life during the Khmer Rouge era was the centerpiece of *The Killing Fields*, a 1984 film that was acclaimed by critics and moviegoers worldwide.

HAING S. NGOR

In 1984, the story of Dith Pran's harrowing experiences in Cambodia under the Khmer Rouge was brought to the screen in the film *The Killing Fields*. Dith was portrayed by Haing S. Ngor, a doctor who had never acted before. Despite his inexperience, however, his moving performance earned Ngor an Academy Award for Best Supporting Actor.

When the Khmer Rouge came to power, Ngor, like Dith, realized that the regime's deep-seated hatred for the educated elite put his life in danger. He adopted the same pose as Dith did—that of a lowly taxi driver. Yet the Khmer Rouge continued to suspect him. Three times, the Khmer Rouge took Ngor into custody and tortured him, demanding he reveal his true identity. They put his head in a plastic bag, sliced off part of a finger, and hit his ankle with an axe, but Ngor still denied his past. Finally, he was able to flee to Thailand, within months of Dith's own escape.

After winning the Oscar, Ngor appeared in a few other movies, most notably the Vietnam War film *Heaven and Earth* (1993). But he spent much of his time lecturing about his experiences in Cambodia. Ngor also helped fund several organizations that provided aid to Cambodians who remained trapped in Thai refugee camps.

On February 25, 1996, Ngor was shot outside his home in Los Angeles, California. Although some speculated that he had been killed by someone with a connection to the Khmer Rouge, three members of a street gang were found guilty of his murder.

and Life of Dith Pran," which was published in the *Times*'s Sunday magazine on January 20, 1980. The article was made into the movie *The Killing Fields* four years later. The film was acclaimed by critics and audiences and seen by millions. Its popularity made Dith Pran the most famous survivor of the Khmer Rouge regime.

Political Turmoil

There was no happy ending for Cambodia during the years of Vietnamese rule. Generally, life was better for the Cambodian people under the Vietnamese than it was under the Khmer Rouge. The mass killings ended. The Vietnamese also allowed many people to return to urban areas and some to attend school and practice their religion. Cambodia's political life, however, remained chaotic. Although the Khmer Rouge was out of power, it was still wreaking havoc. China was supporting it with many millions of dollars worth of aid, and the Khmer Rouge continued to fight a vicious guerrilla war against the authorities of Cambodia's Vietnamese-sponsored government. Two other resistance groups, one headed by Norodom Sihanouk and one led by former prime minister Son Sann, also gained strength.

The Vietnamese relied on funds from the USSR to maintain its hold on Cambodia. But in 1989, with its own economy in shambles, the USSR reduced its aid. Vietnam could no longer afford to stay in Cambodia, so it announced that it was withdrawing troops from the country.

Dith was frightened by the news. He worried that when the Vietnamese left, the Khmer Rouge would once again take over. With this in mind, Dith decided to see Cambodia one last time while he still could do so safely. In the summer of 1989, he accepted an invitation from the Cambodian government, then headed by Prime Minister Hun Sen, to visit the country as a member of the Cambodia Documentation Commission. The commission was dedicated to researching and documenting the atrocities committed by the Khmer Rouge.

When he arrived in Phnom Penh, Dith remembered what the city was like the last time he had seen it: "It was all smoke and noise and fear and confusion." Now its people were no longer living in terror, but Cambodia was still suffering. In an article he wrote for the *New York Times* about his visit, Dith described the widespread misery caused by poverty, bad sanitation, erratic electricity, scarce water supplies, and rampant corruption. He found that most Cambodians were largely uninterested in the warring political factions trying to control the nation. They were far more preoccupied with their struggles just to get through each day.

Just a month after the Vietnamese left, the Khmer Rouge staged its largest military campaign in a decade. In 1991, the United Nations stepped in and negotiated a peace between the four political factions in Cambodia. To enforce its terms, U.N. peacekeepers occupied the country (now officially called the State of Cambodia) for two years. In 1993, Cambodia adopted a new constitution that established the country as a constitutional monarchy, with a king as head of state and a prime minister as head of government. King Sihanouk was restored to the throne, and a prime minister was chosen in Cambodia's first fair election.

The political party led by Norodom Ranariddh, the son of Norodom Sihanouk, won the election. Hun Sen, however, refused to step down as prime minister. Supporters of Ranariddh and Hun Sen hashed out a compromise. Ranariddh became the first prime minister and Hun Sen was named second prime minister. (In practice, Hun Sen ran the government, and Ranariddh's position remained largely ceremonial.)

As Cambodia's government became more stable, the Khmer Rouge began to fall apart again. Many of its leaders left the movement to join the parties of Ranariddh and Hun

"I CRIED EVERY SINGLE DAY"

In the years following the fall of the Khmer Rouge, about 150,000 Cambodians left their homeland to start new lives in the United States. Although each Cambodian immigrant's experiences were unique, many found it difficult to adjust to American society. In the book *Teenage Refugees from Cambodia Speak Out*, a fourteen-year-old named Youeth described her struggles to adapt in her adopted country.

I cried every single day I went to school. Everyone laughed at my clothes because they didn't look right. They didn't like me because I couldn't talk right, my English was so bad. I missed so many classes because I was always crying. It was very bad.

I take care of my parents and grandparents. They don't work anymore since we came here. They are too old. They are very strict and do everything the Cambodian way. They don't want me to go out of the house. I only go out to my classes. If I get a job and go out, my English will get better and I will meet people.

I don't miss Cambodia because it was so bad there. Now I want to be an American.

Sen, which now seemed to have the strongest grip on power. Tensions within the Khmer Rouge over these defections boiled over in June 1997 when Pol Pot, now the leader of the Khmer Rouge, had another important official, Son Sen, killed, along with ten members of his family. (Pol Pot probably suspected that Son Sen would join Ranariddh's party.) Other Khmer Rouge leaders then turned on Pol Pot. They held him under house arrest until he died in 1998. The death of Pol Pot was the beginning of the end for the Khmer Rouge. Within a year, most of its leaders were in the hands of the Cambodian authorities.

Dith Pran was devastated by the news that Pol Pot was dead. As much as he loathed the Khmer Rouge leader, he wanted Pol Pot to live long enough to be charged with and tried for crimes against humanity in an international court. Only when he and the other leading members of Khmer Rouge were tried and sentenced would Dith feel that justice had been done. As Dith explained, "This is sad for the Cambodian people because [Pol Pot] was never held accountable for the deaths of 2 million of his fellow countrymen."

Seeking Justice

Hun Sen, who became the sole prime minister of Cambodia in 1998, was not eager to try Khmer Rouge members. After all, he himself was once part of the Khmer Rouge. In the late 1990s, however, Hun Sen began to rethink his position. International support for the trials was growing, and he feared losing aid from foreign countries if he did nothing. Hun Sen finally agreed to negotiate with the United Nations to determine a structure for a Khmer Rouge trial. In 2006, after many years of talks, they established a special court in the Cambodian judicial system. Formally called the Extraordinary Chambers in the Courts of Cambodia (ECCC), it was to be presided over by five judges—three Cambodian, one Australian, and one Dutch.

REMEMBERING THE KHMER ROUGE ERA

Many foreign tourists in Phnom Penh make a special effort to visit the Tuol Sleng Genocide Museum. The museum occupies the building the Khmer Rouge once used as an interrogation center. Its walls are covered with black-and-white mug shots of the prisoners kept at Tuol Sleng, few of whom survived their ordeal.

Today Cambodians are far less interested than foreigners in visiting Tuol Sleng. Many who lived through the Khmer Rouge era have no interest in being reminded of its horrors. Many younger Cambodians, who were not alive when the Khmer Rouge was in power, know little about that period. Many parents and grandparents, traumatized by what they lived through or guilty about what they did, are reluctant to discuss the era with younger Cambodians. In addition, students are usually taught little about the Khmer Rouge.

In 2007, Khamboly Dy, a young man who worked at the Documentation Center of Cambodia, set out to change that. He wrote *A History of Democratic Kampuchea*—the first book about the Khmer Rouge written by a Cambodian for Cambodian readers. He intended the book to be for high school students, but the government refused to adopt it as an official textbook. It did, however, agree to let schools use it as a supplemental text—a small but notable step forward in Cambodia's struggle to come to terms with the Khmer Rouge era.

Visitors to the Tuol Sleng Genocide Museum in 2008 view pictures of the inmates at the Khmer Rouge interrogation center, nearly all of whom were murdered by the regime.

Cambodians watch the trial of Kaing Guek Eav, the notorious official in charge of the Khmer Rouge's Tuol Sleng interrogation center. In 2010, he was found guilty of the torture and execution of thousands of prisoners.

In late 2007, the Cambodian government placed four Khmer Rouge leaders—Nuon Chea, Ieng Sary, Ieng Thirith, and Khieu Samphan—under arrest. All of them denied any responsibility for the death of 2 million Cambodians between 1975 and 1979. A fifth defendant Kaing Guek Eav, better known as Duch, was also scheduled for trial. He had been in charge of the S-21 interrogation center and had been in the custody of the Cambodian government for more than nine years.

In February 2009, Duch went before the ECCC, becoming the first person ever placed on trial for the horrors of the Cambodian killing fields. Unlike the four other arrested Khmer Rouge leaders, Duch confessed his guilt on March 31, 2009. In the courtroom, he said, "I recognize that I am responsible for the crimes committed. I would like to express my regretfulness and heartfelt sorrow."

This admission of guilt was just what Dith Pran had feverishly hoped to hear from those who were responsible for the Khmer Rouge's heinous acts. But the confession came too late for Dith. Exactly one year before Duch made his statement, Dith Pran had died from pancreatic cancer in New Brunswick, New Jersey.

Known throughout the world as a survivor, Dith sought to honor the victims of the Khmer Rouge by telling others what had happened to them. In a message filmed from his hospital bed during his final days, he explained, "I promised myself, if I survive these killing fields, I would never stop talking about this kind of crisis." Dith kept his promise throughout his life. But even after his death, his story, his words, and his deeds continue to speak. They still demand that no one ever forget the Cambodian genocide, and that no one ever let such a thing happen again.

TIME LINE

1942—Dith Pran is born in Siem Reap, in northern Cambodia.

1953—King Norodom Sihanouk of Cambodia declares his nation's independence from France.

1954—The country of Vietnam is split into North Vietnam and South Vietnam.

1960—Dith Pran begins working as an interpreter for the United States' Military Assistance Command in Cambodia.

1965—The United States launches air strikes on villages along the Vietnamese-Cambodian border; King Sihanouk breaks off diplomatic relations between Cambodia and the United States.

1970—Lon Nol, with the backing of the United States, stages a military coup and takes control of the government of Cambodia.

1972—Dith Pran becomes an interpreter and assistant to *New York Times* reporter Sydney Schanberg.

1975—The United States evacuates the American embassy in Phnom Penh; the Khmer Rouge takes control of the Cambodian capital and government; North Vietnam defeats South Vietnam in the Vietnam War; Dith Pran resettles in a rural work camp at Dam Dek.

1976—Sydney Schanberg wins the Pulitzer Prize for International Reporting for his articles about the fall of Phnom Penh to the Khmer Rouge.

1977—Dith Pran moves to Bat Dangkor to avoid execution by the Khmer Rouge.

1978—The Vietnamese army invades Cambodia after a series of skirmishes with the Khmer Rouge along the Vietnamese-Cambodian border.

1979 —The Khmer Rouge retreats into the jungle; the Vietnamese invade Phnom Penh and take over the Cambodian government; Dith Pran returns to Siem Reap and sees a killing field, then escapes Cambodia by crossing the border into Thailand; Dith leaves Thailand for the United States.

1980 —The *New York Times* hires Dith Pran as a news photographer; the newspaper publishes Sydney Schanberg's article "The Death and Life of Dith Pran."

1984 —*The Killing Fields,* a film based on the experiences of Dith Pran during the Khmer Rouge era, is released in the United States.

1989 —The Vietnamese withdraw from Cambodia, unleashing a period of increased political unrest.

1993 —Cambodia adopts a new constitution and holds its first fair election.

1998 —Khmer Rouge leader Pol Pot dies while being held under house arrest by his former officials.

2006 —Cambodia and the United Nations establish the Extraordinary Chambers in the Courts of Cambodia (ECCC) to try Khmer Rouge leaders for crimes against humanity.

2007 —Four leading members of Khmer Rouge are arrested.

2008 —Dith Pran dies of pancreatic cancer.

2009 —Kaing Guek Eav, the Khmer Rouge commander of the notorious S-21 interrogation center, admits his guilt while standing trial before the ECCC.

2010 —The ECCC sentences Kaing Guek Eav to thirty-five years in prison (sixteen of which had already been served).

NOTES

Introduction

p. 5, par. 2, "killing fields": Sydney Schanberg, *The Death and Life of Dith Pran* (New York: Viking Books, 1985), p. 1.

p. 5, par. 4, "Are you afraid": *The Killing Fields: The Facts Behind the Film* (London: Weidenfeld and Nicolson, 1984), p. 96.

Chapter 1

p. 15, par. 4, "I had not chosen": Ibid., p. 13.

p. 20, par. 2, "I'd give the soldier": Ibid., p. 50.

Chapter 2

p. 27, par. 1, "It's finished": Schanberg, p. 16.

p. 28, par. 2, "They [were] universally grim": Ibid., p. 18.

p. 28, par. 4, "Those who have done": Ibid., p. 19.

p. 30, par. 1, "Bandaged men and women": *Killing Fields,* p. 22.

p. 30, par. 2, "We are not fighters": Ibid., p. 64.

Chapter 3

p. 35, par. 1, "You're a traitor": Ibid., p. 82.

p. 36, par. 1, "To survive": "The Last Word: Dith Pran," *New York Times* video, March 31, 2008, www.nytimes.com/packages/html/multimedia/20080320_DITH_PRAN_LAST_WORD_FEATURE/#section

p. 38, par. 1, "What they were really telling": *Killing Fields,* p. 84.

p. 42, par. 1, "Anyone they didn't like": Ibid., p. 88.

p. 44, par. 3, "You are the enemy": Schanberg, p. 46.

p. 45, par. 2, "He loved me": *Killing Fields,* p. 94.

p. 45, par. 2, "was like a slave": Schanberg, p. 51.

p. 48, par. 2, "All the refugees": *Killing Fields,* p. 96.

p. 50, par. 3, "An American brother": Ibid., p. 108.

p. 50, par. 3, "I am reborn": Schanberg, p. 60.

Chapter 4

p. 59, par. 2, "It was all smoke": Dith Pran, "Return to the Killing Fields," *New York Times,* September 24, 1989, www.nytimes.com/1989/09/24/magazine/return-to-the-killing-fields.html

p. 61, par. 2, "This is sad": Robert D. McFadden, "Death of Pol Pot: The Witness; Survivor of Killing Fields Is Resolute in Quest for Justice," *New York Times,* April 17, 1998, www.nytimes.com/1998/04/17/world/death-pol-pot-witness-survivor-killing-fields-resolute-quest-for-justice.html

p. 65, par. 3, "I recognize that I am responsible": "Khmer Rouge defendant expresses 'heartfelt sorrow,'" Associated Press, March 31, 2009, http://ibnlive.in.com/news/khmer-rouge-defendant-expresses-heartfelt-sorrow/89139-2.html

p. 65, par. 5, "I promised myself": "The Last Word: Dith Pran."

GLOSSARY

ambassador—an official from one country sent to represent its government in another country.

civil war—a war between groups of people living in the same country.

communism—a form of government in which all property is owned by the government and the government distributes goods and money to its citizens.

diplomatic—having the skill of managing the relationships between different countries.

embassy—a building or complex of buildings in which an ambassador and his or her staff live and work.

faction—a small group within a larger group.

genocide—the mass killing of a group of people, particularly a people of a specific ethnic group or nationality.

guerrilla—a member of a fighting force that uses unconventional methods of warfare, usually against a traditional army.

killing fields—areas in Cambodia where the Khmer Rouge slaughtered its enemies during the period when it ruled the country (1975–1979).

malaria—a serious disease carried by mosquitoes.

malnutrition—the condition of lacking the nutrients from food that the human body needs to function properly.

passport—an official government document that states a person's citizenship.

protectorate—a country controlled and protected by another country.

regime—a government in power.

revolutionary—a person who rebels against an established government.

FURTHER INFORMATION

BOOKS

Behnke, Alison. *Angkor Wat*. Minneapolis, MN: Twenty-First Century Books, 2008.

Bergin, Sean. *The Khmer Rouge and the Cambodian Genocide*. New York: Rosen Publishing Group, 2008.

Keat, Nawuth, with Martha Kendall. *Alive in the Killing Fields: Surviving the Khmer Rouge Genocide*. Washington, D.C.: National Geographic Children's Books, 2009.

Sheehan, Sean, and Barbara Cooke. *Cambodia*.(Cultures of the World) New York: Marshall Cavendish Benchmark, 2007.

Weltig, Matthew S. *Pol Pot's Cambodia*. Minneapolis, MN: Twenty-First Century Books, 2008.

WEBSITES

Documentation Center of Cambodia (DC-Cam)
The website of DC-Cam includes essays about the Khmer Rouge period and a database of biographies and photographs of Khmer Rouge members and their victims.

www.dccam.org/Projects/index.htm

***New York Times* Dith Pran Slideshow**
The *New York Times* website offers a slideshow of photographs taken by Dith Pran during his long career with the newspaper.

www.nytimes.com/slideshow/2008/03/31/
nyregion/20080331_DITH_index.html

"Pol Pot's Shadow"
This site, operated by the Public Broadcasting Service (PBS),
features a 2002 short documentary film about Cambodia after
the fall of the Khmer Rouge that originally appeared on the
PBS series *Frontline*.

www.pbs.org/frontlineworld/stories/cambodia/

Tuol Sleng: Photos from Pol Pot's Secret Prison
This website includes a gallery of more than one hundred
photographs taken of Cambodians who were tortured and
killed at S-21 interrogation center (also known as Tuol Sleng)
by the Khmer Rouge.

www.tuolsleng.com/history.php

DVDs

The Killing Fields, DVD, directed by Roland Joffé (Burbank, CA:
Warner Home Video, 2001).

BIBLIOGRAPHY

DePaul, Kim, ed. *Children of Cambodia's Killing Fields: Memoirs of Survivors*. Compiled by Dith Pran. New Haven, CT: Yale University Press, 1992.

Dith Pran. "Return to the Killing Fields." *New York Times,* September 24, 1989. www.nytimes.com/1989/09/24/ magazine/return-to-the-killing-fields.html (accessed April 28, 2010).

Fletcher, Dan. "A Brief History of the Khmer Rouge." *Time,* February 17, 2009. www.time.com/time/world/ article/0,8599,1879785,00.html (accessed April 15, 2010).

Him, Chanrithy. *When Broken Glass Floats*. New York: W. W. Norton, 2000.

Kinetz, Erika. "In Cambodia, a Clash Over History of the Khmer Rouge." *Washington Post*, May 8, 2007. www. washingtonpost.com/wp-dyn/content/article/2007/05/07/ AR2007050701870.html (accessed May 12, 2010).

"The Last Word: Dith Pran." *New York Times,* March 31, 2008. www.nytimes.com/packages/html/ multimedia/20080320_DITH_PRAN_LAST_WORD_ FEATURE/#section (accessed May 8, 2010).

Martin, Douglas. "Dith Pran, Photojournalist and Survivor of the Killing Fields, Dies at 65." *New York Times,* March 31, 2008. www.nytimes.com/2008/03/31/nyregion/31dith. html (accessed May 1, 2010).

McFadden, Robert D. "Death of Pol Pot: The Witness; Survivor of Killing Fields Is Resolute in Quest for Justice." *New York Times,* April 17, 1998. www.nytimes. com/1998/04/17/world/death-pol-pot-witness-survivor- killing-fields-resolute-quest-for-justice.html (accessed April 30, 2010).

Schanberg, Sydney. *The Death and Life of Dith Pran.* New York: Viking Books, 1985.

Schanberg, Sydney H. and Dith Pran. *The Killing Fields: The Facts Behind the Film.* London: Weidenfeld and Nicolson, 1984.

INDEX

factions, Khmer Rouge and,
44–45
families
of Dith Pran, 26, 48, 54
Khmer Rouge and, 37, 38
famine, 42, 44, 48
forced labor, 6, 37–38, 42,
44–45
France, 9, 13, 32–33

government
early history of Cambodia
and, 12, 13
Lon Nol military
government, 15–16, 22,
28, 29, 32, 38
monarchy and, 9, 11, 14–15
post-Khmer Rouge period
and, 58–59, 61, 65
of Siem Reap, 48–49
See also Khmer Rouge
guerrilla warfare, 58

Heaven and Earth (film), 57
Him, Chanrithy, 16
*History of Democratic
Kampuchea, A* (Khamboly),
62
Hun Sen, 58, 59, 61

Ieng Sary, 65
Ieng Thirith, 65
informants, children and, 37
international community
Khmer Rouge and, 37
war crimes trials and, 61

Kaing Guek Eav (Duch),
38, 65
Kampuchea, 37, 48
Khamboly Dy, 62
Khieu Samphan, 65
Khmer people, 12
Khmer Rouge
brutality and, 28, 35, 40–41
civil war and, 21–23
death toll and, 6, 48
factions and, 44–45
fall of Phnom Penh and,
26–29, **29, 34**, 35
Norodom Sihanouk and,
15–16
origins of, 11
post-Vietnamese period,
59, 61, 65
"reeducation" and, 36–38,
39
United States and, 30
Vietnam and, 14–15, 45,
48, 58–59
war crimes trials and, 61,
64, 65
killing fields, **4**, 5–6
Killing Fields, The (film), **56**,
57, 58

land mines, 49
Long Boret, 32
Lon Nol, 15, 16, **18**, 22

malaria, 42
map, **17**
marriages, Khmer Rouge
and, 38

ABOUT THE AUTHOR

Liz Sonneborn is a writer living in Brooklyn, New York. A graduate of Swarthmore College, she has written more than eighty books for children and adults. Her works include *Vietnamese Americans, The End of Apartheid in South Africa,* and *A to Z of American Indian Women*.